On The Bench

– ELINA LISA –

An environmentally friendly book printed and bound in England by www.printondemand-worldwide.com

Mixed Sources
Product group from well-managed forests, and other controlled sources
www.fsc.org Cert no. TT-COC-002641
© 1996 Forest Stewardship Council

PEFC Certified
This product is from sustainably managed forests and controlled sources
www.pefc.org

This book is made entirely of chain-of-custody materials

www.fast-print.net/store.php

ON THE BENCH

A catalogue record for this book is available from the British Library

ISBN 978-178456-025-6

First published 2014 by
FASTPRINT PUBLISHING
Peterborough, England.

╬

I'm sitting on that bench,
And laughing at the moon
It's getting cold,
But still I cannot move

I'm scared if I do,
The spell will be broken
So I'm sitting here in the dark,
The only sound coming from the beats
    of my heart

Maybe with childish hopes
I'm waiting for that star to fall,
And burn those half-collapsed bridges
Which have led me here.

Don’t shut that door when leaving
I like to feel that feeling,
The feeling to be in the middle
With one leg here, but
with the other already in the future

I love that in-between time
Like a half of just-cut lime,
Half of a dime,
Half of just-spared time

With the part of me in the past,
Well knowing that’s not going to last
Kind of expecting next,
But not quite sure what’s for
  the best

Learning to enjoy that time in the middle,
Not looking back or forwards either
With every doubt for future, for past
We have to take it and make it to last.

I'm hearing footsteps by my door,
I'm waiting for that shadow on my floor
Listening to wind, to leaves, to the breeze,
Every sound still makes me freeze

Though I know I have to let go,
I have to stop something beginning with the
letter ... to play,
But I just can't get you out of my mind
Every sound, every smile I still rewind

The harder I try to escape,
The more you seem to want to stay
It's difficult to live with,
But even more so to leave....

╬

Strange autumn once I had
Tell me where it went,
Strange events passed by
Oh, don't ask me how did they end

Don't ask me why
Trodden grass is still trying to spring,
Don't ask me why
There is no answer to all the world's whys

Strange whirlwind once blew by
Tell me, where did it whizz to
Strange train I once jumped on
Tell me, when and how did it crash

Don't ask me why
I still try to figure things out,
Don't ask me why
There is no answer to all the world's whys.

Did talk to you this morning
Wow, your voice was so full
of not caring,
Like I'm just another stone
you throw in the puddle,
God, how did I ever get so
muddled

Now I promised myself
to be strong
and noticed my ability to trust
has gone cold
I doubt every word that is said
And keep my mind to my-
self.

Now though it's a little bit sad
Life with the red alert always on the blink
But life is a lesson, so they say,
And sure for me, always bloody
maths seems to be on.

Where have they gone, those childhood days
When my biggest worry was –
how to throw a stone,
To try to catch that snowflake on my tongue
Knock on neighbours' doors and run

Though I didn't appreciate it back then,
Now I would give up a world to be 10
Let someone else take all the worry and care,
And go back in time, when to jump in the
largest puddle was my biggest dare!

Someone today said to me,
That I've got the saddest eyes they've ever seen
I thought to myself - Oh dear, how can this be,
Even my pretend smile can be seen through

You know when sometimes you look up to
the sky,
And feel like someone on you has put that
bad eye
No matter what you seem to do,
You always manage to strike a lose

Now I sit here and with so-called sad eyes
look at the flame,
With thoughts going through my mind -
What life has become.

This morning at a rainbow I'm looking,
Which gently is in my hair reflecting
And then again, I feel like a teen,
Which seems I was just last week

Wish I could go bare-foot,
And run and run till all my worries stopped
Then that warm hug of Mum's I miss,
That strong shoulder to lean against

And still I wish for a carefree day,
Please give me one, just please one more ...

Then in the moistness of dew I'm peeking,
Where I can see the hidden truth -
That I'm not any more that teen,
Which seems I was just last week.

Oh why, oh why
Myself – again to sleep I cry,
Feeling of breaking
  seems to be so deep,
With every day, you hope
 it will get better, but that
  feeling seems to keep

When I feel like that and
my mind gets overstressed,
I wish I could talk to you,
because you would know what
  I intended

I still talk to you, though
  it's in my mind
And I would give up a
  world
To hear your sensible
  voice

But now you have gone
  and can't be reached
No matter how hard I
  pray or plead,

But still I keep talking to
you in my mind
However, of course, it's just
not the same.

╬

Flip a coin –
Heads I lose,
Tails for the
same move

I flip first for you,
Second for me and a few
others just because

They're still in the air,
Haven't landed yet,
So I close my eyes
in a moment of seize

I hear the noise of
them hitting the ground,
Open my eyes to give a
glance
Two have gone missing
And by chance,
one is spinning on
its side

It seems strange
that coin can't decide –
Heads for the lose or
tails for the same move.

I believe they did it at last,
Wouldn't put it past –
They have turned the light off,
the light at the end of the tunnel

I thought it's just me, and I again
Can't see things straight, but
It doesn't feel like that, this
time around

Been informed the economy in
the country is no leisure, so they
had to take on new measures

So now we all sit in the dark,
though some might think:
"Oh, it's my time to depart", but
no, it's not like that at all and it
doesn't really matter how this
time, things turn out, at least we
can blame it on the government.

Being lonely in a crowded street,
Smiling so wide, though my inside screams
Why does it seem to be the story of my life -
Even when something good happens, it's
    like a wolf as a sheep in disguise

Really don't know how this can be,
Maybe it's my way up to Purgatory -
Who knows how long it could be and
how did I manage to get here

Though I walk it, I do hope it's a mistake
And I've been made to take someone else's
    place.

When a new day is beginning
With the dawn and birds there singing,
Give us your help, we ask, we plead
In every step, give us a lead

When another day we are living
Millions of things to achieve, we are trying,
Give us your helping hand, we ask
Make our moans a thing of the past

When again this day is closing
And for a better tomorrow, we are waiting,
Give please your comfort in our hearts
So each day could be a new, fresh start.

Wish I could live a day,
One like my last
Wish I could live a life,
So there are no regrets

So fulfilled is every moment,
And shines out of each of the smiles
When you shut the door behind you,
You still can hear a goodbye sigh
When closing the cover of a book,
Wind still blows the leaves back

I want love – tell out loud and
  not to keep quiet
I want every note – sing out
  like a new song
I wish the good that is inside me
Not to hide, but share,
So you people who hear me -
Also take your part.

I'm living with a scar in my heart
In this world so wide,
So wide and dark
So empty and cold,
Where you cannot see light
        Or an exit close by

I walk around with a scar in my heart
It's been so deeply etched in my chest,
It hurts so badly
Every time I take a breath,
And carry along on my everyday path

I am in this world which seems so endless
So close and so far at the same time,
So misunderstanding, so misleading
With the scar in my heart, I must live in it.

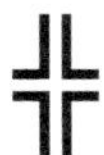

So many thoughts,
So many ideas and dreams
So many what ifs seem to
  be going around

So many silly mistakes,
So many dreams whilst
  you are awake
And a million unanswered
  questions too

So many bits of everything,
Seem to be going around -
Little bits of you lost in this
  mighty unknown,

Though the only thing that seems
  to be missing -
Is the truth in your words
  when asked -
How you are feeling?

When one autumn day
I am looking out at the rain,
And all my emotions, feelings
With it seem to go down the drain

I don't know where is more storm,
Out there or inside my brain
And no matter where I turn,
All I seem to do is crash and burn

I'm desperately trying find that light
    at the end of the tunnel,
But even hope for it somehow seems
    to be doomed
And though I have lost all my believing,
    I still go to bed -
Pleading for something to brighten
    my morning.

Seems I'm playing Russian roulette,
Sitting with closed eyes and waiting
 For the bullet
Part of me, scared to take this test,
But the second, anxious and intrigued
 What happens next?

I'm sitting in the silence and not
 daring to breathe,
And like mad heads spinning
 in distress

You don't know how hard this
 bullet of life will hit you,
But you have no choice just to
 accept it is coming.

I was stargazing tonight
Thought there weren't any stars to gaze at,
I was watching a candle burn this eve
Thought there weren't any candles burning

I have been daydreaming again,
Which has replaced my dreamless nights
I have been trying to put ahead my steps,
Though for each one I take, two seem to
    be going back

All my rights I try to do seem
To go crashing on the rocks,
And despite it all, I'm still urging to believe -
there must be hope left in Pandora's box.

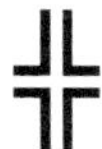

Got an arrow shot right
through my heart,
Tried to fix the hole, but it's
still apart

Have tried it all - super glue,
tape, even Blu Tac, but
though the hole had been mended
it's still badly scarred

All I need is for you to come
Place your hand on that
painful wound
And like magic, I truly
believe - the scar in my heart
will disappear.

I trusted we could win this fight
No matter how hard its bite,
Feels like we got shot before leaving the field
So here we lay on the ground – I've got an
  injured heart, you mind

We had been split in the recovery ward,
And I'm not sure, will we forever be apart
So there we are, we met in the battlefield
  and by an explosion got burned

I wrote you a note and sent it with the dove,
but before it got there, you were already gone.
Now I keep it close to my wounded heart,
and forever wonder why we met at war.

I will stop trains in their tracks,
I will try to block ships from leaving docks
I will run, I will jump, I won't sleep
Even if it is just spending an hour with you

There is nothing that would stop me,
There is nothing that could faze me
I'll be there in seconds,
If only we could have one more moment

My coat is by my door,
My shoes next to it on the floor
Just give me a sign that you are waiting somewhere,
And I'll be ready to depart.

Silence is awful, silence is hard
It takes you and rips right from the heart
Words can be cruel, words can be harsh,
but silence and unsaid can rip you apart
Though sometimes they say that
    silence is gold,
In my opinion, it's the coward's way out.

Feel like I'm fighting a losing battle,
Running like a just-released herd of cattle
Biggest problem is I don't know where
I'm heading,
With my head spinning and heart
racing

I know that you all say it's just a state
of mind -
And sure mine isn't at all right,
But I just don't seem to be able
to cope
Have lost even the last grasp of hope

Senselessly running down the street in
the middle of the night,
No matter what I start, it all seems to go
wrong
You all say it will be fine, it all just takes
time,
But even on better days, I don't believe
time is on my side

I'm scared like a small child, but I wont
show it or say it out loud,

I will wait and see as I always do,
Though I do that - believe it's not easy
for me.

╬

I had a phone call this morning
Again, they tried to sell me double glazing,
I tried that polite approach,
But still they didn't seem to get the gist

I even told them that I live in a den
And don't have a single window to see the sun,
They said "Oh, we can make you one and as an
extra, provide insulation as well"

I thought to myself – for crying out loud,
Is that really something that
should be allowed?

In the end, here I sit today,
With a window and insulation for
everyone to give on Christmas day.

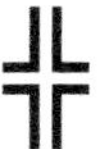

I was trying to count those sheep,
So I could faster fall asleep
They were big and small,
  active and calm,
Some had lost their heads
and were very berserk

I was trying so hard, but
lost my count and when
I got back on track, they all
 seemed to be catnapped

So I lie here in the quiet
    and dark,
With no sleep coming to greet
and around me is a full flock
    of asleep sheep.

When you feel like breaking into a million pieces,
And you put on the mask even to familiar faces
Can't help, but tears stream down your cheeks,
And wish your mind could be replaced

Your wide-eyed stare right at the ground,
With hope that this will soon be behind
When you feel like you've been over this so many times,
All echoes you get are from your loud cries
There is only one thing that helps you out,
Hope that tomorrow will come out bright.

I don't believe it's that much to ask
Just a little sleep if that's ok,
Had enough of counting cows, dogs
  and sheep
For crying out loud it's nearly 3

And how dare my neighbours sleep,
When I can't, my eyelids shut to keep
I sway my glance at that shelf,
Heck, let's mix some zopiclone with the wine

Of course I know what my doc would say,
But the less he knows, better sleep, so to speak
So let's now enjoy some rest,
But please keep this tip a secret.

Would want to talk about Christmas,
And the closeness, and calm, and the smells
Wish I could talk about hopes and for
That magic which everyone waits

But somehow, thoughts are not going there,
And my soul, like an injured animal growls
When the axe which chops your festive tree,
Seems to make a bigger wound in my soul

Not sure I can find that magic
Though it still must be somewhere,
But somehow, in a moment of eye blink
Again it seems to pass me by.

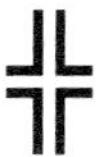

I laugh so I won't have to cry,
I'm still holding on though my
grip is slipping

Morning has broken yet again,
Another heavy day without the sun
I realize that this time I'm not just
bent, but I am broken,
No matter what ladder I climb on,
On the last step, I seem to be slipping

So I lay here on the ground so close to
my point of breaking,
And it feels like when I'm down I also
get the worst kicking

I close my eyes, count to three
I so wish at last I could be free,
But yet again this time it doesn't
feel like it's happening,
Though I still lay here and hope
at the point of landing.

Another prisoner on
death row,
Without the will to plea for pardon
I'm counting my days and nothing
seems to make any sense,
Just waiting for someone to read
my sentence

Another row sitter asks - how did I get here?
I look at my chained arms and
legs and say – it has been a cruel fate

And then there are others who
seem to come and go,
All of them expecting
release before their time

Only I somehow seem to be stuck -
Still counting my days and
waiting for that luck.

Why do older people
stop in the shop aisles,
And start chatting, not
moving for ages?

When you go with your
shopping and in a speed,
You suddenly get stopped by the
"mild and the meek"

All my sympathy goes right to
them,
But this one has never made
any sense

Even stranger is to understand,
That no matter what aisle I
Pick, they are already there

How can this always be,
Sometimes I think they are
hunting for me.

I'm on the seventh floor high,
Standing by a window open wide
Staring out at the empty air,
Which seems to be betting for me
to take the dare

Another what if is coming to mind,
Life in my brain seems to play on
rewind
I take a deep breath and close my
eyes,
Three jumps of my heart over skips
the pulse

I don't know why,
But this time I step away
Leaving the spot where I was standing
behind –
And thinking will I be as strong
when next time arrives.

By the side of the lake I sit,
By the side of the lake I wait,
I have packed and stay day or night,
I am here, I will never quit

Looking in waters where my
  dreams are swimming,
Gazing in reflections, taking breath and
  listening to my heart beating

I step closer to feel the stream,
I touch the wetness and it becomes me
Make a splash and with it a single wish,
Can feel the chill and now it's part of me

I take a step back and then again closer,
I feel that wetness and it becomes me
Let's make a second wish and the third will
  be for free ...
Take the step back, and then again closer,
Feel the chill and now it's part of me ...

I came to meet you,
You were never here,
Standing on that street corner
with rain crying down

It's like heaven opening
and being part of this,
Never expected, never understood,
never forgotten ...

Though I'm still standing with
The downpour on me and
I can hear laughter coming
down from above

And now I'm leaving and
I won't be coming back,
just came to say my goodbye
as I'm ready to depart

I walk through the city,
the same streets I know,
the same villages and
    even faces

Though I'm sorted, I feel
 a little bit sad
because I know I won't
 be coming back

Just wanted to say good-
bye while I still can,
Though none of you
were here when I did, I
believe you heard and
 felt it inside.

They say you've still
got it all – if you've got hope,
But I suppose you still have to know
what it looks like and where it lies

Maybe on occasion, it could come
like a gentle bear to give you an embrace,
But then again, it could turn out to
be a bitter truth which slaps your face

You can never know its shape or form
  or where it could hide,
Maybe it could be so close and even
  part of your brain

It could be a small insect which buzzes
  around your head,
Or as big as that prince on a white
  horse still hiding in the shade

It should not matter where, how
  and the way it's hiding -
But apparently you're alive whilst you've
  still got it.

With a big passion
I went today for confession
After an hour telling my story,
Never heard someone laughing
so endearing

He said "My dear you have given me
some Christmas cheers,
But let's now get to the serious parts"

I told him that I was not joking,
However he never seemed to stop
that unconvinced smiling

Though then he said I will give you
my forgiveness,
To what, I shrugged my shoulders and
responded - I just wanted to talk, but
there is no regret in my heart.

That innocent look in your eyes,
That embarrassed smile on your face
Oh, I so wish it could have been truth,
And I hadn't fallen for these cheap games rules

So yes I should have known better,
But your buttered words were
so smooth,
Still I look and feel very bemused

You hit me like a train running at speed,
Drove right over and left me on the ground
to bleed
And yes again I should have known
better,
At least now I've got injuries as a reminder.

Feel like a beggar sitting on the corner
of a street
By an empty bowl, I sit here and weep
No, I'm not asking for crazy treasures,
Just a little peace of mind would be a
pleasure

Maybe a crumb of joy also wouldn't
go amiss,
Or understanding why my life has
taken such a twist
Seems like I've been kneeling here
forever,
With the sky above rapidly turning
greyer

Passing people giving me their blank
looks,
The ones I betted my life on seem to
be triggering guns

I turn to them hoping that at least
they would shoot -
Oh why, oh why has my life taken such
a turn,
A future in a fading robe -
Is what I can see to be my only run.

They say that you've only got
one real love in your life,

But how to go about it if
both of you have not been
given a chance,
Or one of you has been struck by a
lightning shot,
But maybe the world hasn't brought
you to the same spot,
Or so-called fate has torn you apart

Would that really mean that you have
lost your second half
And now for the rest of your life
You will just have to find someone
to fill the hole

And you go and interact and try to get
through, but still suppose you
have that question of doubt in
your mind.

Like the last apple on that tree,
Still hanging in autumn's breeze
So many winds, so many frosts,
But still clinging on with the last
    strength of the stalk

Passing people giving it a glance,
And we are all aware that it's only a
    matter of time,
The last apple will eventually give,
But for now it's still holding, still
    hanging in the breeze.

What's the point of tens of happy hours,
If none of them bring you any happiness?
What's the point of hundreds of falling stars,
If none of them fill a single wish?
What's the point of thousands of dancing snowflakes,
If none of them are hitting the ground?
And what's, yes what's the point of a million dreams
If you are not in any of them?

╬

I'm taking a walk down to
the beach tonight,
Thought it's quite cold and
close to midnight

I'm walking and counting the
footsteps I take,
as many sand grains as I
can sense

Been watching seagulls
passing me by and
little marks in the sand they
leave behind

I also hope that the next ones
who will walk along,
Maybe will see spots of me
left by the banks

And I guess as time passes by,
There will be more people
taking their footsteps along
and counting as many sand grains
as they can.

Not quite sure if there are any remarks to make about my last poem:

It's a shame that it has to be this way,
But this seems my only way for a gateway
Please all I ask is don't judge when I leave
And know this is my time to be free

I believe I know what you would say
  and think,
But guess I just don't fit herein
And all I plead of you just once more,
Please don't judge, I loved you all so
and you have meant the world to me ...

ND - #0160 - 080726 - C0 - 197/132/3 - PB - 9781784560256 - Gloss Lamination